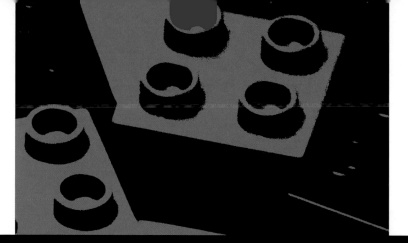

Can You Guess What I Am?
At Home

J.P. Percy

A+

Smart Apple Media

How to use this book

This book combines the fun of a guessing game with some simple information about familiar objects at home.

Start by guessing
- Carefully study the picture on the right-hand page.
- Decide what you think it might be, using both the picture and the clue.
- Turn the page and find out if you are right.

Don't stop there
- Read the extra information about the object on the following page.
- Turn the page back—did you miss some interesting details?

Enjoy guessing and learning
- Don't worry if you guess wrong— everyone does sometimes.
- Your guessing will get better the more you learn.

I have teeth, but I can't bite. Can you guess what I am?

I am a zipper!

Zippers were invented to join pieces of cloth together. They can be made from metal or plastic. The tiny parts that lock together are called teeth.

We help you make colorful pictures. Can you guess what we are?

We are pencils!

The first pencils were made over 400 years ago. The insides were always gray. Today, pencils can be made in every color of the rainbow.

You might find me in the kitchen. Can you guess what I am?

I am a kiwi fruit!

Kiwi fruit is soft
and good to eat.
The black dots inside
are seeds.

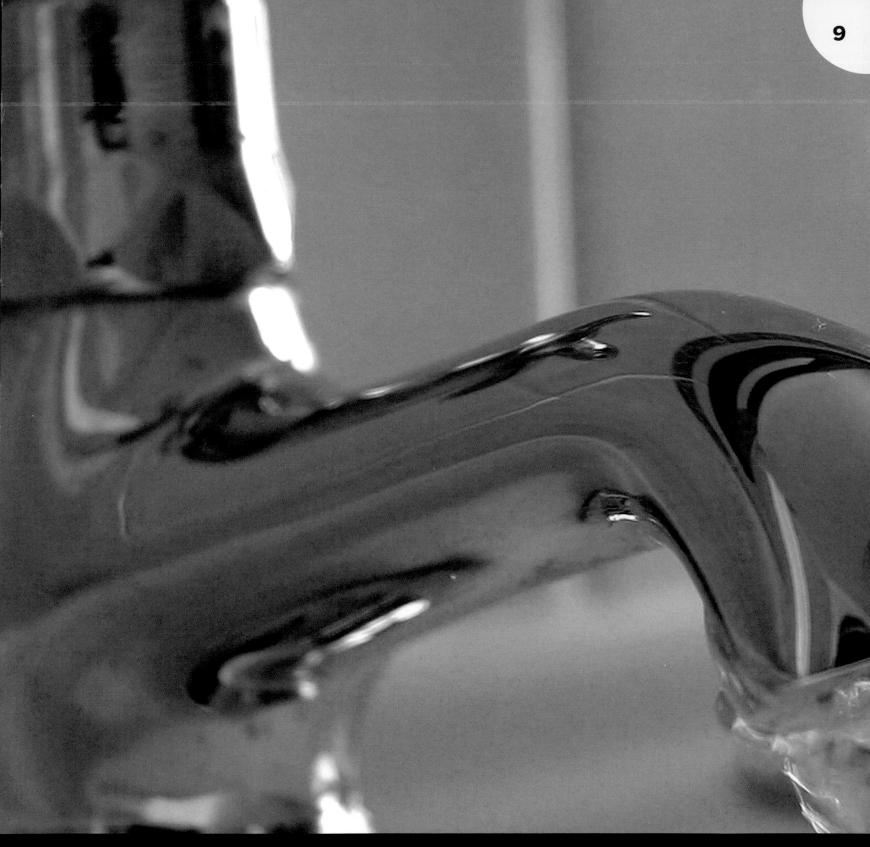

I can run hot and cold. Can you guess what I am?

I am a faucet!

It is easy to turn on a faucet to get water. To reach your home, water may travel for miles in pipes.

You might use me when you are eating. Can you guess what I am?

I am a knife and fork!

Knives, forks, and spoons can be made from metal, plastic, or wood. In China and Japan, people use wooden sticks, called chopsticks, to eat with.

I like to float in a bubble bath. Can you guess what I am?

I am a rubber duck!

Rubber ducks are usually found in your bath at home. In some countries, people have duck races, called duck derbys. Lots of rubber ducks are put in a river and people watch them race to the finish line.

I have hands and a face. Can you guess what I am?

I am a clock!

Clocks have two hands. The small hand points to the hour and the big hand points to the minutes.

I go up and I go down. Can you guess what I am?

I am a staircase!

Stairs help us to climb up and down in our homes. The longest staircase in the world has over 11,000 steps!

I am soft and cuddly. Can you guess what I am?

I am a teddy bear!

Teddy bears are named after a famous American president. His name was Theodore, but some people called him Teddy. Teddy bears are fun to snuggle up with when you go to bed.

Now try this...

Make it!
Make a patchwork picture of your favorite teddy bear or other soft toy. Glue lots of scraps of fabric onto a piece of paper. On the back of the paper, draw the shape of your teddy bear. Cut out the shape. To make eyes and a nose you could glue buttons on.

Guess it!
Collect some objects from around the house and mix them together in a pillow case. Make sure you don't put anything sharp or wet in it! Play a game where one person at a time puts their hand inside the pillow case, feels an object, and then tries to guess what it is.

Eat it!
Eating fruit and vegetables is very good for you. Ask an adult to help you make a fresh fruit or vegetable salad. To make it even more fun, you could try eating it with chopsticks instead of a knife and fork!

Published by Smart Apple Media, an imprint of Black Rabbit Books
P.O. Box 3263, Mankato, Minnesota 56002
www.blackrabbitbooks.com

Published by arrangement with the Watts Publishing Group LTD, London.

Library of Congress Cataloging-in-Publication Data
Percy, J.P.
At home / J.P. Percy.
    p. cm. — (Can you guess what I am?)

 Summary: "Use the hint to help you guess which household object is pictured in the close-up photograph. Turn the page to see if you are right and to learn more about the object!"—Provided by publisher.

 ISBN 978-1-59920-893-0 (library binding)
1. Picture puzzles—Juvenile literature. I. Title.
 GV1507.P47P47 2013
 793.73—dc23

                            2012033093

Series editor: Amy Stephenson
Art director: Peter Scoulding

Picture Credits:
a40757/Shutterstock: 17, 18. Anteromite/Shutterstock: 7. bluecrayola/Shutterstock: 13. brieldesign/Shutterstock: 8. Carlos Caetano/Shutterstock: 15, 16. Joe Gough Shutterstock: 9, 10. Jiri Hera/Shutterstock: 11, 12. Karuka/Shutterstock: front cover tl. lilly3/istockphoto: 3, 4. Loskutnikov/Shutterstock: front cover tc, cl, cr, bc, back cover tl, tr, bl, br. Suzanne Tucker/ Shutterstock: 2, 22. 26kot/Shutterstock: front cover tr, 5, 6. Chepko Danil Vitalevich/Shutterstock: front cover br. Michal Vitek/Shutterstock: front cover bl. Jason Walsh/istockphoto: 19, 21. Jamie Wilson/Shutterstock: 14.

Every attempt has been made to clear copyright. Should there be any inadvertent omission please apply to the publisher for rectification.

Printed in the United States of America at Corporate Graphics in North Mankato, Minnesota
PO1586
2-2013

9 8 7 6 5 4 3 2 1